The 365 Days of Christmas

Keeping the Wonder
of It All
Ever Green

William J. Byron, S.J.

To Diane Driscoll —

Christmas peace!

Wm J Byron

Paulist Press

New York/Mahwah, N.J.

Library of Congress Cataloging-in-Publication Data

Byron, William (William J.)
   The 365 days of Christmas / William J. Byron.
     p. cm.
   ISBN 0-8091-0481-4 (alk. paper)
   1. Jesus Christ—Nativity—Sermons. 2. Christmas—Prayer-books and devotions—English. 3. Christmas sermons. 4. Catholic Church—Sermons. I. Title.
BT315.2.B97 1996
242'.33—dc20
                                      96-16618
                                         CIP

Cover design by James Brisson

Interior illustrations by Daisy de Puthod

Book design by Kathleen Doyle

Published by Paulist Press
997 Macarthur Boulevard
Mahwah, New Jersey 07430

Printed and bound in the
United States of America

Contents

*For my sister-in-law Marta
whose year-round generosity
is especially evident to
all the Byrons at
Christmastime*

Acknowledgments

M y thanks to the Byrons, McNierneys, and Gillins for making Christmas so memorable for me over the years; to Walter J. Burghardt, S.J., for introducing me to Saint Augustine's Christmas and Epiphany sermons; to the academic community at The Catholic University of America for ten annual pre-Christmas concerts, liturgies, and celebrations on campus; and to the Jesuit Communities at Wernersville, St. Louis, Woodstock, Loyola in Maryland, Loyola of New Orleans, Scranton, Holy Trinity in Georgetown, and Georgetown University for past and present Christmas joy.

On many Christmas Eves, I've celebrated the Eucharist in the Rosemont College Chapel for parents, students and staff of nearby Sacred Heart School in Bryn Mawr, Pennsylvania; some of these reflections originated in that setting.

"Peanuts, Emeralds, and the Art of Giving" appeared in slightly altered form in *America* magazine, December 24, 1977.

Scripture quotations used here are from the *New American Bible,* Copyright 1991, The Confraternity of Christian Doctrine, Inc. All rights reserved.

Preface

Although Christmas comes but once a year, it doesn't have to go away. The Christmas spirit, once grasped, can be, quite literally, the "gift that goes on giving." An understanding of the deeper meaning of Christmas can stretch around the clock and across the calendar for a full twelve months, for three hundred and sixty-five days of difference in the life of any believer. The problem, of course, is how to plant within oneself the deeper meaning of Christmas.

This book helps to address that problem. The planting starts at Christmastime. If the roots sink in, the spirit of Christmas can remain, green and growing, all year long.

Curious, isn't it, that the typical Christmas tree has no roots. It is cut fresh, decorated brightly, placed on a stand, and left to dry out slowly in just a couple of weeks. Christmas trees are expensive and beautiful, but they just don't last. That is exactly what happens in the minds of millions who pack away the meaning and memory of Christmas with the ornaments every year. They remain unopened for fifty weeks. If, however, the meaning of it all is planted in the soul, in the ongoing life of the mind, there is a difference. The Christmas spirit, like a deeply rooted Christmas tree, can flourish, without the tinsel, all year long.

These reflections are assembled here for remembrance and reflection on the part of those who love the Christmas story and want not only to hear it anew each December, but to ponder its implications throughout the year. This book is smaller than most books and larger than most Christmas cards. It fits comfortably in the in-between places, like coat pockets and Christmas stockings, and can be opened in those in-between times from January to November. It can bring Christmas to July and fill quiet moments with Christmas thoughts in every season of the year.

These musings emerged from my own Christmas-season reflection, prayer, preaching, and academic scribbling. They are intended to enhance the year-round meditative moments of contemporary Christians, who might be ready at any time to catch a glimpse of the deeper meaning of it all.

WJB
Georgetown University
Christmas, 1996

So many of those who unreflectively repeat "Merry Christmas! Merry Christmas!" have no appreciation of who Christ is, and was, and will be forever.

ONE

"In the Beginning..."

It would not be difficult to make the case that the sad-dest line in all the literature of the world is this one verse from the prologue to the gospel of St. John: "He was in the world, and the world came to be through him, but the world did not know him." The prologue refers to him as "the Word"—"In the beginning was the Word, and the Word was with God, and the Word was God." He, God, came into a world full of persons who owed their very existence to him, and yet they did not recognize him for what and who he was.

And the very next verse drives the same point quite lit-erally home, to his very own people—"He came to what was his own, but his own people did not accept him."

Those words used to be read at the end of every Mass, every day, in what the Catholic world referred to as "the last gospel." They underscore the tragedy of lost opportunity for those who neither recognized their Creator nor welcomed their Savior when he stepped into their history, and not their history only, but into their human nature and human flesh.

But St. John goes on, in the same prologue, to relate the very good news that "to those who did accept him he gave power to become children of God."

He, of course, is the Christ of Christmas—Son of God, Second Person of the Holy Trinity. And just as this prologue contains one of the saddest sentences in all literature, it also contains one of the most sublime—*Et Verbum caro factum est,* "And the Word became flesh," *et habitavit in nobis,* "and made his dwelling among us," or, as the Greek words in the scriptural text so graphically express it, he "pitched his tent among us."

When you consider that the Word of God took human flesh, your flesh, can you be anything but reverential toward all human flesh? Can you have anything but respect for the human body knowing, as you do, that God chose to have one for himself? The Divine Word became human flesh in the body of a virgin who brought him into the world for all to see. He was in the world, he who had made the world, but the cold, preoccupied world of the first Christmas morning did not recognize him.

Had he presented his plan for salvation and evangelization of the world to be critiqued by "event managers," or "media advisers," or "public relations consultants," they might have said, "Fine, begin the dramatic revelation in swaddling clothes, hidden away in a manger, cared for by a maiden-mother and strong, silent carpenter. Fine to be surrounded by shepherds and livestock, cut off from the world in a cave. But don't wait too long to break out of obscurity, to overcome those humble origins and impress the world with some display of power and might. Lay out your plan for maximum primetime impact. Force the world to listen."

This, of course, was not the way he chose to proceed. He did step into a public life, but he waited three decades to do so. He performed some miracles when he became a public figure, but he always remained hidden—disguised, you might say—in human flesh. He preached and taught, but always in human tones and simple words. And, after a very brief public life, he died, an apparent failure, in humble circumstances, on a cross of wood no harder that the wood of the manger, thus tracing out from wood to wood, from hardship to hardship, not just a way of life, but a map of life to be picked up and followed by those who want to be like him.

And even when he rose from the dead and completed his mission by establishing his church, he forced no one to belong to that church; he compelled no one to follow him. Just as he had come into a world that knew him not—did not recognize him—so he left a world that, for the most part, still did not know him, still failed to recognize him.

Fortunately for us, however, the meaning of Christmas and the mission of Christ were not lost on all. Think of those earliest of Christians who did recognize him, who did believe, and think of those who preserved that belief and handed down that faith over the years to you. Be grateful to them and to God for this great Christmas gift—belief in the divinity of Jesus Christ, your Lord and Savior, who was there "in the beginning," the Word. "All things came to be through him, and without him nothing came to be."

Along with gratitude in your heart, make room for a certain uneasiness, a restlessness rooted in a sense of pity and concern for those who still do not recognize him. So many people in your world, in your own city and neighborhood, do not know Christ. So many of those who unreflectively repeat "Merry Christmas! Merry Christmas!" have no appreciation of who Christ is, and was, and will be forever. They deserve a place in your Christmas prayers; they also deserve to have a chance to see Christ in you every day of the year.

Those who say, "Let's put Christ back into Christmas," make a worthwhile point, but they have also to reflect on the antecedent necessity of putting Christ back into the heart of every Christian. The warm appeal of the Babe of

Bethlehem and the attractive personality of the man he grew up to be are dimmed, not highlighted for the world to see, but dimmed by the absence of Christ-like living in those who claim to know, love, and follow him.

Among Christians there are those who do not, in fact, receive him, who really do not recognize him hidden as he now is, not in his own human flesh, but in eucharistic bread and wine. Pity his own who do not recognize him in the breaking of the bread.

The Christian heart is large and expansive on Christmas Day. There is room there for overriding joy to accompany the pity produced by a reflection on the tragedy alluded to in the prologue, a tragedy not unlike that of a child, separated in infancy from a parent, who in adulthood passes that parent on the street, each oblivious to the identity of the other. But the overriding joy is there for anyone who believes, whose heart knows the gratitude that St. John's proclamation of Word made flesh is intended to produce.

Open up your eyes to the beauty of the original Christmas scene, and your heart to the profundity of the Christmas mystery, and let your heart be filled with joy, a Christmas joy intended for every believer. Even if you don't feel it now, because of temperament or circumstance, pray for the Christmas gift of a deep abiding Christmas joy in the realization that God is with you, will always remain faithful to you, and will never stop offering you the gift of salvation. That is the ultimate message of Christmas.

Some overlooked dimensions of Christmas joy were incorporated into the Christmas sermons of St. Augustine—the joy, for instance, of virginity preserved for the sake of the Kingdom, the joy also of chaste living in or out of marriage. In consequence of the Incarnation, the Christian faith teaches, there is reproduction in the order of grace for all who unite themselves with Christ. Rejoice, therefore, Augustine would say, in the birth of new grace in the world whenever you unite your will to God's will, as Mary did; whenever—by recognizing, and accepting, and believing in him—you permit him to empower you with the power of Christmas for the salvation of the world. "In the beginning was the Word, and the Word was with God, and the Word was God. He was in the beginning with God. All things came to be through him, and without him nothing came to be. What came to be through him was life, and this life was the light of the human race; the light shines in darkness, and the darkness has not overcome it."

In this reality, in this profound mystery, lies your deepest Christmas peace.

*Christmas is a time to think anew about life,
and promises, and other sacred things.*

Two

The Sacred Things—A Christmas List

Nothing's sacred anymore," you might find yourself saying, along with countless others, whenever scandals break, idols fall, and news of violated integrity makes the headlines. A glance at the entertainment menu the nation seems to like would also make you wonder. And you get disappointing and disillusioning news occasionally from family and friends, news that doesn't find its way into print, but gets around nonetheless on the "have-you-heard?" circuit and leaves you let down, and sad, and asking yourself, "Isn't anything sacred anymore?"

Yet you know deep down that a lot of things are indeed sacred and still widely regarded so. You would be letting yourself down (and your nation too) if you failed to take stock of those sacred things from time to time. Simply listing them—privately and personally, or publicly for others to review—is one small preparatory step toward the personal and public recommitment required for the preservation of all things sacred. Christmas is a good time for this kind of reflective exercise.

Any list along these lines will, of course, be partial. Most lists will be highly personal and quite particular. Anyone's list, yours included, can be a model—a do-it-yourself kit—for others who might be willing to pause and take inventory of the things they would never trifle with or trade away. These lists could produce the stuff of great conversations within the family circle at Christmastime.

Our world with all its private and public parts was quite imperfect on the first Christmas Eve; it still is. It could be better. It would be better, I believe, if it were less littered with broken promises. So "promises" would be high on my Christmas list of sacred things. Marriage vows, religious covenants, and faith commitments are the promises I would most want to protect. But the list could easily run on to include treaties, contracts, and agreements that hold human relationships together in other important areas of life.

Life is sacred, human life first and foremost. At every stage of growth, decline, and demise on the way to eternal life, human life is sacred (all contrary evidence from news reports and the world of entertainment notwithstanding). The widespread disregard for the dignity of human life and the wanton destruction of human life on our planet are shockingly evident to those who really believe that human life is sacred. The absence of shock would signal the presence of insensitivity to the sacredness of life, particularly to life embodied in fetal or less-than-perfect forms. Something sacred is inextricably present in persons who are weak, poor, homeless, diseased, or aged. Unattractive persons, unpleasant persons, hostile and unforgiving persons—all, because they are persons, are sacred. This perspective comes more readily, perhaps, at Christmas than at other times of the year, even though all things sacred remain sacred every day of the year.

So, "promises" first, "persons" second in this particular catalogue, although the primacy always belongs to person, the producer and protector of promises.

Once "life," embodied in persons, and "promises," specified by the persons who make them, are on the list, it will become evident upon reflection that all other things sacred are extensions or expressions of these two basic and especially sacred realities.

"Home" is sacred, of course, because it shelters another sacred reality, "family." It is easy to make the case for that at Christmas. Both home and family serve life. Both follow upon the promise that made the marriage that produced the family that settled in the dwelling place called home.

Sex is sacred because life is sacred. And, as both literature and life attest, sexuality without the promise gives the lie to human love, another sacred reality. The inclusion of sexuality on the list of sacred things is a welcome reminder that not everything sacred is necessarily solemn.

Freedom is sacred because without it life cannot enjoy full expression. One's homeland can be considered sacred and worth defending because life has taken special shape there, culture has developed there, security of person and family are rooted there.

Professional responsibilities are sacred, especially when they flow from promises made, and when those promises relate to life-sustaining, life-protecting, and life-enhancing activities.

Space, when set aside for religious reasons, becomes sacred. Church, synagogue, mosque, temple, shrine: the space is sacred because it is dedicated to a purpose that recalls a promise—God's promise to be forever faithful, God's promise of salvation.

Trusts are sacred. When something is entrusted to someone, it becomes a "sacred trust" if so regarded by those conferring and receiving it. Here your list could become quite personal. Whether public trust or private, a promise is always involved; so is a determination to keep that promise, as we often put it, "so help me God."

Christmas looks to life—the fullness of life with family

and friends, the promise of life eternal. Christmas is the fulfillment of a promise. For Christians who believe, and for all others who respect the Christian faith commitment, Christmas is a time to think anew about life, and promises, and other sacred things. Failure to reflect from time to time on all things sacred will guarantee the arrival of a day when "nothing's sacred anymore." The sacred things will have been traded or trifled away.

When gifts are unexpected and also recognized as being totally undeserved, they ignite both joy and surprise. They can never bring disappointment, just a pure happiness free of any discontent. Would that it worked this way for all of us at Christmas.

THREE

"A Gift Is When You Get Something You Don't Deserve"

'Twas a day or two before Christmas when *The Wall Street Journal*'s front page presented this cascading headline to its readers:

Better to Receive
How Children Decide
On Gifts They Want,
And Plot to Get Them

———

After All the TV Watching,
Playground Talk Crowns
The Cool and the 'Dorky'

———

Art of Manipulating a Parent

———

The story, with a Dallas dateline, focused on ten-year-old Dan Chenoweth: "This time of year, everything that seems important to [him] can be found, row after colorful row, in a suburban toy store." With due acknowledgment of the influence of television advertising, window-shopping, and schoolyard story-swapping on this youngster's consumer preferences, the *Journal* noted their derivative and decisive influence on "how his father, Jeff Chenoweth, spent the $250 he budgeted for his son's Christmas."

How big is the business impact of such decisions? "Collectively," this news story explains, "the 28 million Americans ages six to 13 will get more than $10 billion in toys this Christmas, setting another record for an industry that hasn't suffered a slump in 30 years."

About twenty years ago, I celebrated a Christmas afternoon Mass in my brother's home, surrounded by a circle of my nieces and nephews and other children of close friends. They were all in that 6-to-13 age range. Earlier on that Christmas Day, much earlier, the same living room where we gathered for the liturgy had been littered with gift wrappings and ribbons cast aside as presents were torn open in wide-eyed delight. When evening drew near and we gathered to listen to familiar scripture readings before offering our gifts of bread and wine to God in Eucharist, I made a catechetical attempt to connect the celebration of God's original Christmas gift to us, in the person of Jesus, with the gift-exchange that brightened the early hours of Christmas Day.

"What's a gift?" I asked of no one in particular in what passed for a "dialogue homily" during the liturgy of the word. (Family Masses at home were a familiar holiday tradition for these children; they didn't enjoy being "called on," as we reflected on the scripture readings, but they usually spoke up on their own in lively discussion of the texts.) "What's a gift?" I asked again.

"A gift is when somebody gives you something," replied a nine-year-old, proving once again that children of that age will invariably define something in the exact terms of that which is to be defined.

"All right," I responded, "a gift is when somebody gives you something. Now suppose I borrowed a dollar from you last week and now I'm returning it. Here. I'm giving you a dollar. Is that a gift?"

"No, that's no gift."

"But you just told me, 'A gift is when somebody gives you something,' and here I am giving you a dollar. Why isn't that a gift?"

Silence.

After a long minute, another youngster spoke up: "A gift is when you get something you don't deserve!"

With an expression of thanks for the insight, I was able to go on to say a word about our "giftedness," and original "undeservedness," and thus our reason for joy and gratitude on Christmas Day.

I reinforced the point about gratitude by explaining to these children that when their fathers and I were young devotees of Saturday afternoon cowboy movies—"Westerns," as more sophisticated film buffs later came to call them—the cowhands we and our friends idolized and imitated usually said "Much obliged" in situations where city folks would have said, "Thank you." Naturally, we would repeat that sample of Wild West vernacular at our respective supper tables on Saturday evenings: "Much obliged, Ma'am," as the mashed potatoes were passed around.

This remembrance provided me with an opening for two final catechetical points: the word "eucharist" means thanks, and that for which we give thanks at Christmastime—the gift of our salvation in Christ Jesus—brings with it an obligation, a condition of being "much obliged" to share our lives and gifts with others as a way of saying thanks to God. The "thankssaying" to God is a "vertical" acknowledgement of our debt and dependency; the "thanksdoing" for neighbor is a "horizontal" expression of what it means to be "much obliged." With that we moved our Christmas Mass on to the offertory, eucharistic prayer, communion, and the possibility of subsequently viewing any gift received as something undeserved, a perspective that first prompts gratitude, and then conveys an obligation to share with and do for others. "The Mass is ended, go in peace to love and serve the Lord," is an invitation to the believer to go out and try to put this Christmas theory into Christian practice.

It is unlikely that Dan Chenoweth, or the two nine-year-olds, Sara Campbell and Willie Marshall, who were also featured and pictured in *The Wall Street Journal* story, would be immediate converts to my point of view on Christmas giving and receiving. Willie's mother, according to the *Journal*, "views Christmas as a way to reward her son for shunning the drugs and crime of a rough neighborhood. When planning her splurge, Ms. Marshall commented, 'I'm determined to get Willie what he wants....His father has never been around, and Willie doesn't let people get close to him. He deserves it all. He's a good boy.'"

In a paragraph directed to the business reader, the news story notes: "While adults have become more value-conscious in the 1990s, children haven't left the 1980s. One recent study shows that although 70% of adults are now big buyers of private-label store brands, only 7% of the children would consider the stuff; they want brand-name gifts and designer clothes. Brands offer children a common commercial language, something identifying them as part of the group. Nonbrand items or those at discount stores are suspect." Nine-year-old Sara Campbell is *The Wall Street Journal's* witness: "Things that aren't on sale are better." Sale items are "on sale because people want to get rid of them."

Don't expect her to understand what you mean, if you should decide to repeat the old saying: "It's the thought that counts." That kind of counting just does not add up for today's child. When gifts are unexpected and also recognized as being totally undeserved, they ignite both joy and surprise. They can never bring disappointment, just a pure happiness free of any discontent. Would that it worked this way for all of us at Christmas. It would be so much more consistent with our celebration of the reception of the gift of the Messiah, who was expected but undeserved, and who came in "swaddling" not designer clothes, and in wrappings without any label at all.

Gifts to others in the family are often artful and even expensive dodges enabling one to avoid or postpone the gift of self. True understanding of the other means understanding the other's need. True love means self-giving to meet that need.

FOUR

Peanuts, Emeralds, and the Art of Giving

Gift shops, almost by definition, stock ample supplies of things no one really needs. And gift-giving, especially at Christmastime, is often less than satisfying because the gifts that most of us select have a curious way of missing the point. The gifts that may come to mind—those carefully chosen, perhaps expensive gifts, neatly wrapped and hidden, or only recently presented—may be hindering rather than helping the goal of true gift-giving, which is an expression of love.

Sadly, family gift-giving all too often bears out the description of the average marriage given by a psychiatrist in T.S. Eliot's "The Cocktail Party": "Two people who know they do not understand each other,/ Breeding children whom they do not understand;/ And who will never understand them." Gifts to others in the family are often artful and even expensive dodges enabling one to avoid or postpone the gift of self. True understanding of the other means understanding the other's need. True love means self-giving to meet that need. With this in mind, I invite the reader to run through a gift-list review.

Begin by considering a gift from wife to husband.

Think of husbands-in-general and simply disregard their different sizes, shapes, and ages, their income, health, and hobbies. Those incidentals and accidentals only get in the way of fundamentals: fundamental needs and fundamental gifts to meet those needs.

Deep in the heart of any husband is a keen sense of his success or failure as a man. If he is like the vast majority of other men, his tendency is to focus, with the inward eye at least, much more on his failures than on what others might reasonably consider to be his successes. He wants to be a leader at home, at work, in the community. He wants to be a successful provider, an effective lover. Yet he knows how infrequently he enjoys genuine success. His opinions are seldom sought out. The scope of his influence is not very wide. Despite what may be a handsome, smiling, self-assured exterior, he is frequently a silent sufferer at the hands of emotional fatigue, frustration and—the word is to be noted carefully—discouragement. In moving language, Carl Sandburg caught this human condition with the words: "Those who order what they please/ when they choose to have it—/ can they understand the many down under/ who come home to their wives and children at night/ and night after night as yet too brave and unbroken;/ to say, 'I ache all over'?" That "husband in general" frequently "aches all over" with discouragement. What gift does he want from his wife? A great deal of encouragement when he is weak, and approval when he is strong.

In our society, a man tends to live much of his greatness when he is away from his wife. His successes almost always occur away from home. But when success fades or vanishes—as it usually does—it is normally only his wife who sees him tired, worn down by competition, frightened by his failures. She should respond with the needed love and encouragement. Women participating in this gift-list review (many of whom, of course, also enjoy significant successes in the world of work away from home and husband) might mark this down: approval and encouragement. Give it. And say it. As the Bible so wisely reminds anyone with sense enough to listen: "Better open reproof than voiceless love" (Prv 27:5).

Next, a gift from husband to wife. A wife, too, lives much of her greatness away from her husband. She may be holding a job outside the home and/or managing a household and young children, with all that implies in terms of balancing professional responsibilities with home economics, child psychology, household nursing, and neighborhood diplomacy. She appreciates compliments on her meals and household management and will happily return them to a spouse who assumes his fair share of those responsibilities. But she wants and needs a whole lot more.

The wife-in-general has womanly fears of being unloved or even unlovable. She has a fear of being considered unattractive. And, more often than most men would suspect, she is beset with a gnawing sense of loneliness. Her husband must try to understand her need and learn to give her considerate, attentive, and affectionate love, just as she must learn to give him encouragement. Loneliness constitutes the need. Considerate, attentive presence meets that need. So check it off on your gift list, gentlemen: considerate, attentive, affectionate love. And underscore it with that biblical verse: "Better open reproof than voiceless love."

Notice how well the exchange of gifts works out. If each is concerned about the need of the other, each is likely to find his or her own need met. It is easy for a man to be affectionate to a woman who gives him constant encouragement. But turn that encouragement into constant criticism and just watch the gap between them widen. It is easy for a wife to encourage a husband who is warmly affectionate.

But turn that affection into disregard or, worse, disrespect, and the consequences cannot be anything but bad. Anyone with even a casual exposure to literature or life knows how those triangular situations can develop when the gifts just listed are not freely exchanged between husband and wife.

Next on the gift list are items for the children. A child's most basic need is security. It amounts to the same thing to say the child needs the certainty of being loved. Someone once wisely remarked: "Every child has the right to be an only child for at least five minutes a day!" A child needs constant praise and encouragement. An advertisement some years ago spoke comparatively of baby food and daddy food. The point of the ad escapes me now, but I think it is worth noting that there is a relationship between baby gifts and daddy gifts. Growing boys need a lot of encouragement; your growing girl needs some antidote to loneliness.

As they grow a little older, into the early teen years, youngsters need a great deal of approval and understanding from their parents. Most parents should probably treat their teenage sons and daughters a little more like adults, criticize them much less, listen to them much more—a happy home is a place where everyone listens—and encourage them constantly. In the early teen years, a boy or girl must face the terrible test of being accepted or rejected by equally insecure peers who often deal with one another capriciously and unfairly. They have a burning desire to belong, to be liked. No son or daughter wants to be pushed by parents into social settings where he or she might be hurt or embarrassed, but children do want the quiet backing, trust, and patient understanding of their parents. No parent has ever known for sure the exact point where trust ends and neglect begins. So, understandably but unwisely, most conscientious parents come up short on trust while tightening up on control.

Peanuts, Emeralds, and the Art of Giving

In her famous diary, Anne Frank repeated a saying that she personally treasured: "In its innermost depths, youth is lonelier than old age." Parents should remember this as they make their gift-list review. They would be shocked to learn how many young people actually hate themselves, and startled to realize that this condition is the result of a childhood endured without genuine parental affection. Gifts to the young should never be the bribes parents all too readily offer. Nothing less than self-donation is required of parents to meet their children's needs. Frequently, the measure of this will be time. Make a gift of time to them. In the process, a child will receive something more: a sense of affirmation and self-worth.

As America grows wealthier and increasingly preoccupied with comfort, our gift-list revision might benefit from the advice given to a young mother by Robert E. Lee. Lee's biographer, Douglas Southall Freeman, recounts the story this way: "Had his life been epitomized in one sentence of the book he read so often, it would have been the words: 'If any man will come after me, let him deny himself, take up his cross daily and follow me.' And if one, only one, of all the myriad incidents of his stirring life had to be selected to typify his message, as a man, to the young Americans who stood in hushed awe...as their parents wept at the passing [of his funeral procession], who would hesitate in selecting that incident? It occurred in northern Virginia, probably on his last visit there. A young mother brought her baby to him to be blessed. He took the infant in his arms and looked at it and then at her and slowly said, 'Teach him he must deny himself'" (*R.E. Lee: A Biography,* Volume IV, Scribner's, p. 505). This lesson is a necessary gift that parents in affluent America are becoming progressively less capable of presenting to their sons and daughters.

Little more than a word is needed here—but that word

will be important—to discuss gifts from children to parents. If the gift exchange between parents goes well, and if parents' gifts to children meet the genuine needs of the young, the young in turn will learn what true gift-giving is all about. Still a word will help, and that one word is "reverence." It is my suggestion that children of all ages should give their parents reverence. Most of us will have to search rather deeply in experience and perhaps consult a dictionary to find the meaning of that word, for the reality of reverence is falling out of fashion now. Its restoration in practice will be a gift to enrich American culture as well as the lives of those who gave the gift of life.

In any case, reverence belongs on the gift list. Its presence there could represent an act of enlightened self-interest for the one drawing up the list. If it is true that "beautiful young people are accidents of nature and beautiful old people are works of art," those who are not yet old might benefit from the reminder that it takes work to make a person an attractive target for the reverence of the generation just coming up on the other side of the hill. From young to old, the gift is reverence.

Now, what about gifts and giving for the single adult, the widow, the widower, the divorced parent, the irreconcilably estranged spouse? What about those who are neither husband, wife, parent, nor youngster? All women must face the problem of loneliness—and, to a lesser extent, discouragement. All men must come to terms with discouragement—and, to a lesser extent, loneliness. Discouragement and loneliness beset everyone. If there is no husband or wife to give the needed gift, where will it come from? Anyone in this situation will know what one man meant when he commented, "When Adam was lonely, God didn't create for him ten friends, just one wife." When there is no one to give the needed gift, where will it come from?

Well, for those whose gift-list looks toward Christmas, there is an obvious answer to that question. The Christian believes that Christmas marks the birth of the final answer to the deepest human need. For Christ came to heal all wounds, even the wounds of loneliness and discouragement. To the Christian eye, the "Word made flesh" is not only a Savior but a Divine Person. Hence, Christ, the original Christmas gift, is truly a gift, representing, as he does, the gift of self, the divine self, to us. And, to the Christian ear, the words "Christ our Savior is born" mean a gift has been given, an exquisite expression of divine love.

For others who believe, but not in Christ, holiday gift-giving is often part of a celebration of a feast of lights. Their gift brings brightness into the lives of others.

Possession, in faith, of the God who reveals himself as one who loves and enlightens is a gift available to all who believe. This gift is more than adequate for those who have no immediate human support in the face of the basic needs that underlie the gift list I've developed in this reflection. Here is a summary of that list. From wife to husband: approval and encouragement. From husband to wife: considerate, attentive, affectionate love. From parent to child: security, affirmation, affection, time, and patient understanding. From sons and daughters of all ages to their parents: reverence. From God to all of us, especially those of us who have to go it alone: the gift of never really being alone but always having within us divine life, light, and love.

And, because materialism often tends to mar our gift-giving and getting, it might be profitable to end these reflections with the familiar and true story of the enduring romance between journalist-playwright Charles MacArthur and the great actress Helen Hayes. When they were young and about to be married, Mr. MacArthur bought Miss Hayes a bag of peanuts, presented them with a flourish, and said,

"I wish they were emeralds." Years later, as Charles MacArthur was dying, he gave his wife an emerald bracelet and said, "I wish they were peanuts."

To a great extent, the secret of successful gift-giving depends on the ability to keep the value of both emeralds and peanuts in perspective.

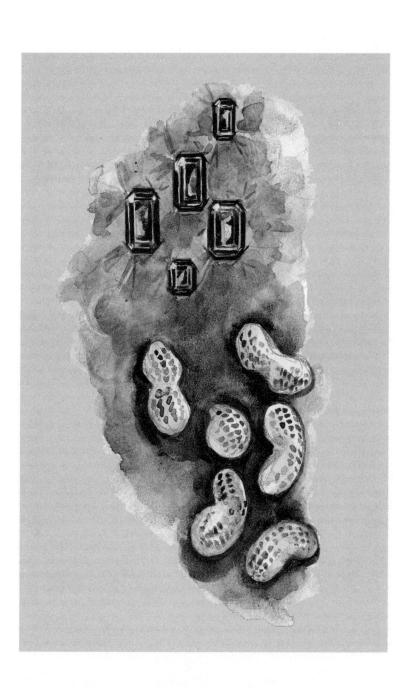

We Christians are surface celebrators; we back off from the shattering truth of the mystery of Christmas. We refuse to believe that Christmas is quite literally a reduction to zero. And, refusing to believe, we are unable to teach or practice the wisdom that is wrapped in the pages of the Christmas gospel.

FIVE

Christmas Is Reduction to Zero

There comes a time," wrote Mahatma Gandhi, "when an individual becomes irresistible and his action all-pervasive in its effect. This comes when he reduces himself to zero."

In my view, not Gandhi's, the Christmas mystery is the greatest and, therefore, the most irresistible and all-pervasive reduction to zero the world has ever known. God emptied himself and the world was filled with a new spirit, a new power, a new life. "They name him Wonder-Counselor, God-Hero, Father-Forever, Prince of Peace. His dominion is vast and forever peaceful...." Thus the prophet Isaiah describes the ideal Davidic king (Is 9:6). His eternal rule shall be assured by the Lord of hosts. The fulfillment of this promise, according to Christian tradition, is embodied in Jesus Christ.

Lodged as they are at the heart of one of the most important messianic passages in the Old Testament, Isaiah's words are proclaimed each year throughout the world at the midnight Christmas liturgy. "His dominion is vast and forever peaceful." This the Christian believes. And yet the Christian knows that the dominion of Christ does not, in fact, extend to every human heart; the peace of

Christ is absent from many men and women and nations around the world.

Why is his dominion not wider? Why is his peace not more widely shared? Because, I think, we Christians are surface celebrators; we back off from the shattering truth of the mystery of Christmas. We refuse to believe that Christmas is quite literally a reduction to zero. And, refusing to believe, we are unable to teach or practice the wisdom that is wrapped in the pages of the Christian gospel.

Christmas invites us to ponder our own reduction to zero. Self-consciously, we can begin by considering how we relate to an infant—any infant. Infants know they are all need; they do not indulge themselves in the luxury of pride. They are open; infants have no adult prejudices. They are open to learning any language, liking any skin color, adapting to any culture.

Less self-consciously, perhaps, we can try relating to Christ as infant. He is not now an infant; we know that, of course. But we might discover our own distance from zero, if we try relating to him as an infant. Anyone capable of relating to a child is on the way to zero. Such a person is not too tangled up with systems, procedures, honors, prejudices, property, and pride.

St. Paul urged something of the reduction-to-zero wisdom in his Letter to the Church at Philippi (2:3-8):

> Do nothing out of selfishness or out of vainglory;
> rather, humbly regard others as more important
> than yourselves, each looking out not for his own
> interests, but [also] everyone for those of others.
> Have among yourselves the same attitude that is
> also yours in Christ Jesus,
> Who, though he was in the form of God,

did not regard equality with God as something to
    be grasped.
Rather, he emptied himself,
taking the form of a slave,
coming in human likeness;
and found human in appearance,
he humbled himself,
becoming obedient to death,
even death on a cross.

Now there you have a description of reduction to zero!

Jesus himself gently prods us toward the practice of
this wisdom with the words, "...unless a grain of wheat falls
to the ground and dies, it remains just a grain of wheat; but
if it dies, it produces much fruit" (Jn 12:24). The riddle of
the grain of wheat, the paradox of finding through losing, of
gaining through giving—all the gospel "contradictions" and
value-reversals are hidden there in the Christmas mystery.
This is the reduction to zero that releases the power of peace
so that his dominion will indeed be "vast and peaceful forever." Is Isaiah's promise still believable?

A pondering and probing of the mystery of Christmas
might open our eyes just a bit to the fact that our God is a
God who was willing to be reduced to zero. His Christ—his
anointed one—is the zero in whom and through whom and
with whom God's kingdom, power, and glory are with us.
And our pondering and probing may open our hesitant
hearts to the truth that we who follow Christ in this world
are men and women who are called to lose our lives in order
to find them, to reduce ourselves, or be reduced, to zero so
that the power of God can move through us to touch a tired
world. That is how Isaiah's promise of vast dominion and
unending peace will be fulfilled.

Christians are men and women transformed by Christ

and conformed to him, not conformed to the world in which their transformation takes place. Christians are not, however, called to shun the world. Nor are they called to a passive, conflict- free existence. Reduction to zero liberates the Christian to build and even battle in a world filled with intractable problems that impede the pervasiveness of the peace of Christ. The problems are evident: men and women the world over oppressed by war, by want, by hatred and injustice; institutions in need of reform; social structures and systems in need of new directions, if not a new creation.

Jesus, the Divine Person with whom the Christian must try to relate as zero to zero, once spoke of himself as "the one whom the Father has consecrated and sent into the world" (Jn 10:36). And so it is with every Christian. The Father sends him or her—consecrated, made holy (let the Christmas "holly" remind you, as the word was intended to suggest, that you were made "holy"!) by the grace of Christmas—into a world in need of healing and help. But in order to help, the Christian must, like God himself, accept a reduction to zero.

This is the truth that separates the surface celebrators of Christmas from the true believers.

Perhaps these ponderings on the mystery that is Christmas will suggest some ways of measuring one's progress toward zero. Improvement in the art of listening—active listening, especially in the family—might be a sign of progress. Improvement in the art of receiving—receiving from others gracefully, instead of trying to dominate others by one's own bribe-like giving—would be another measure of progress. True, it is "in giving that we receive," but receiving gracefully is in turn a gift to the giver. Or, acceptance and practice of the principle that no gain will be taken at the expense of another might be a good indicator of progress toward zero. Whatever the norm, the reality being measured is progress toward that time "when an individual becomes irresistible and his action becomes all-pervasive in its effect."

This is the promise of Christmas. Its price is reduction to zero. Refusal to pay that price keeps peace beyond our grasp. And yet, every Christmas kindness is a sign that a believing world is making quiet progress toward the promise of Christmas, toward Christian zero. The spectacle of Christmas simplicity and generosity is enough to keep hope alive, a hope that finds its own words to praise the rescuing love of God for all who believe.

Modern men and women have cause to claim a peace that is not complacent, a joy that is not naive. To the extent that this is explainable, the explanation lies in the power of Christmas.

SIX

Light and Darkness

Stirring words from the great prophet Isaiah ring out in song and solemn proclamation across the Christian world throughout Advent and the Christmas season. Worshipers assembled for Christmas Midnight Mass will, for instance, hear him say:

> The people who walked in darkness
> have seen a great light;
> Upon those who dwelt in the land of gloom
> a light has shone (Is 9:1).

Regrettably, those who hear these ancient words today can regard one another now, centuries after these and all the other words of Isaiah were spoken, as fellow dwellers in the land of gloom. The human condition, we are tempted to say, has not changed all that much over twenty centuries of war, and want, and selfish disregard for the rights and needs of others. But Christ's birth has changed the human condition, we know; it is just that the supporting evidence for this assertion of Christmas faith is rather hard to find. All the more reason, then, to reflect anew on the power of Christmas—a power that disperses darkness and gloom. This reflection is needed, I think, if perspective is to be achieved, balance maintained, and hope restored in our age of ambiguity.

Isaiah spoke of a "people who walked in darkness." His phrase is fairly descriptive of humanity without Christ, who is, of course, the light of the world. The prophet described those people as "dwelling in the land of gloom." Christian tradition has repeated these prophetic expressions down through the ages for the precise purpose of celebrating the dispersal of darkness and the lifting of gloom by the coming of Christ who is forever our light and joy. And yet the reality of darkness and gloom somehow persists in us, and around us, so that for some of us the Christmas celebration has a hollow ring; it is somewhat forced and unconvincing.

Every Christmas is celebrated in an "anno Domini," a "year of Our Lord." How can the Lord's year, any year, be a year of gloom? Jesus is Lord, but never a Lord of gloom! Quite the opposite. Under his lordship, gloom is destroyed forever and a joyous peace is available to all who believe. Perhaps that gloom—undeniably present in so many human hearts, in different circumstances, places, and periods of history—is a measure of our distance, as a people, from him. To be a dweller in the land of gloom is to refuse somehow submission to his loving lordship. That submission is not easy.

Sad to say, on any Christmas you can look around and see suffering and death, violence and decay, fear and anxiety, hatred and injury. You can see broken promises and smashed hopes. There is reason enough to feel gloomy on Christmas Day or on any of the other 364 days of Christmas.

But you also see around you goodness and love, generosity and trust, service and life, hope and faith. You see covenants kept and you see fidelity in all its forms at work to keep the human community on course. Modern men and women have cause to claim a peace that is not complacent, a joy that is not naive. To the extent that this is explainable, the explanation lies in the power of Christmas.

Power in any circumstance is the ability to cause or prevent change. God's power has changed us. The human race once walked in darkness; we now have access to the light. But we too have power. Each human person is powerful enough to resist the change from darkness to light. "And this is the verdict, that the light came into the world, but people preferred darkness to light, because their works were evil" (Jn 3:19). When the human person is powerful with a power that is not of God, he or she condemns himself or herself to walk in darkness. But when empowered by faith and divine love, the human person can disperse the darkness and lift the gloom.

The power that generates the darkness of violence and hatred, of greed and grinding fears, often resides in institutions, in the ways we have of doing things. Of human creation, there are in any society institutional arrangements that contain but do not harness power—institutional arrangements that fail to reflect the goodness of persons in that society who are transformed in Christ.

The power, on the other hand, that communicates love and faith among humans is the power of persons whose transformation into Christ enables them to find in their human weakness the strength to support one another.

If you put your total trust in structures, you may find yourself walking through darkness into the land of gloom. If you put your trust in persons, you may be deceived and let down once in a while, but you may just find yourself walking in the light. Perhaps our land is one of so much gloom because we find it easier to use the words "fidelity" and "trust" when we name our banks and insurance companies than when we deal directly with one another. But that's where the power of Christmas is at work and where the light is to be found—in one another.

It has been remarked by one who knows the fourth gospel well that John the evangelist writes the way Rembrandt paints—all in tones of light and darkness. In the fourth gospel, those who come to Jesus are in the light; those who turn from him walk in darkness.

Imagine a group of believers coming out of the midnight darkness into a church for Christmas Mass. If they were to turn their faces outward, away from one another, and look through the walls, so to speak, they would experience the darkness, even perhaps a sense of gloom. But let them turn toward one another with smiles of recognition in a circle of warmth and trust, and they will generate a light that suggests a presence and a power in their midst. Human kindness is a revelation of the divine. God is there in their midst.

Christmas lights on trees and roofs, and in the windows of our homes, communicate a warmth and welcome to the beholder. But the Christmas light in the face of the believer says so much more. It repeats the message of Paul to Titus: "For the grace of God has appeared, saving all and training us to reject godless ways and worldly desires and to live temperately, justly and devoutly in this age..." (Ti 2:11). The offer is irrevocable. "Jesus promises you two things," a wise and humorous priest I knew liked to remind anyone he met: "Your life will have meaning, and you're going to live forever. If you can find a better offer, take it!" Now that "the grace of God has appeared," you need not walk in darkness nor dwell in the land of gloom.

This message is *readable* for anyone who picks up the New Testament. It is *audible* wherever the gospels are proclaimed. And it is intended to be *visible* in the life of the believer. This is the power of Christmas. This is light in our world today.

St. Bernard wrote that there are three distinct comings of the Lord: his coming to humankind, offering salvation to all; his coming *into* us, a spiritual presence; and his coming *against* the human person, where the human person prefers the darkness to the light. Christmas celebrates Christ's coming to and also into us in the sense of John 14:23: "Whoever loves me will keep my word, and my Father will love him, and we will come to him, and make our dwelling with him." If we love him and welcome him, we need not fear his coming against us.

For us the darkness has ended; the land of gloom has been left behind. What was written centuries ago in the Letter to the Ephesians remains true today:

> For you were once darkness, but now you are light in the Lord. Live as children of light, for light produces every kind of goodness and righteousness and truth. Try to learn what is pleasing to the Lord. Take no part in the fruitless works of darkness; rather expose them, for it is shameful even to mention the things done by them in secret; but everything exposed by the light becomes visible, for everything that becomes visible is light. Therefore, it says:
>
> > "Awake, O sleeper,
> > and arise from the dead,
> > and Christ will give you light" (Eph 5:8-14).

Each Christmas celebration is a remembering that we were once lost, irreversibly so, from the standpoint of our ability to do anything about it, but now we are found.

SEVEN

A Christmas Parallelogram

Here is an invitation to let the imagination stretch, an opportunity to sketch mentally a spatial framework within which the earthbound mind can follow the traces of the Incarnation. I never read science fiction, so my vocabulary is innocent of any hidden motive when I say I have four directional forces in mind; they can be labeled Horizontal I and Vertical I, Horizontal II and Vertical II. No cryptic symbolism is intended (if you see two crosses, they are in the mind of the beholder, not part of my scenario). I'm thinking only of a few trajectory lines designed to focus attention on the reality of creation, sin, incarnation, grace, and redemption. The dimensions of this reflection may appear to be ambitious, and they are, but Christmas fosters an expansive mood that I want now to indulge.

The opening chapter in this book recalls St. John's gospel-opening declaration and provides our only possible point of departure: "In the beginning was the Word." This sentence echoes, of course, the very first words of the Bible—Genesis 1:1: "In the beginning, when God created the heavens and the earth...." There (but where was "there"?), with the Father and the Holy Spirit, was the Word—from the beginning.

"All things came to be through him, and without him

nothing came to be," relates the evangelist as his gospel begins to unfold. In, at, of, from the beginning, lives a triune God who decided in, at, of, and from the beginning, to create. Moving horizontally (Horizontal I), in a manner of speaking (intended only to keep the imagination fixed on a state of being before the fall from grace), the creative love of God produced an Adam, then an Eve. The two stood together in a position parallel (apart from, off to the side, by no means equal) to their Lord and Creator, but graced with divine life, divine familiarity. There they stood in their innocence, in God's presence. Freely and foolishly, however, Adam and Eve turned away and lost themselves. They fell "downward," if you will, into another level of existence where it was impossible for them to find their once familiar God. It was the first ever "free-fall"; it was a vertical drop (Vertical I).

At this lower level of unfamiliarity, on this plane of alienation, were and are born the descendants of Adam and Eve whom God "had banished from the garden of Eden" (Gn 3:23). "Between us and you a great chasm is established..." the Lord God might have said, as did Father Abraham in Luke's famous parable (Lk 16:26); and he might have added, as did Abraham, that the chasm is fixed "to prevent anyone from crossing who might wish to go from our side to yours or from your side to ours." But God had other plans—from the beginning.

The infinite goodness of the triune God that prompted the decision to create also prompted the decision that the Second Person of the Trinity, the Word, should become man—step down into human flesh and human history (Vertical II) in order to close the chasm and find the lost human race. Because of the fall, we lost humans had, in St. Augustine's words, nothing "whereby we could live," while the Word, not yet incarnate, had nothing "whereby he could die." So, in a mysterious celestial exchange, God became human so that humanity could be reinstated in the family of the Trinity. In that eternal decree from our triune God, the death of the Son of God was mysteriously and inextricably linked with life for every son and daughter of Adam and Eve. The Incarnate Word, the Son, would become the anointed one, the messiah, the Christ, whose death would redeem (the word, of course, means "buy back") the fallen human race.

Thus from all eternity, divine wisdom set the path that Christ would trace through the human condition toward death (Horizontal II), so that all who would believe in and follow him might themselves move through death to life. That is what baptism—a sign, a symbol, a sacrament that effects what it symbolizes—does. It plunges (that is what the verb "to baptize" means) you symbolically into the death (recall the death-dealing potential of water) of Christ, so that you can rise (out of that symbolic death) with Christ to walk in newness of life.

When Christ was born, he moved, so to speak, off the plane of the Creator-Lord and down to earth. As man, he walked the earth inviting the lost to be found, offering sight to the blind and health to the sick as "signs" affirming his universal offer of salvation to sinners. He searched out the lost human race collectively by a covenant sealed with his blood; he searches out each human person in every age and every place, individually, by the stirrings of grace, by whispers to the heart, by bidding each to come, to follow him back to the Father.

Into this Christmas parallelogram, this imaginative spatial framework for considering the dimensions of Christmas, I like to insert words written by Karl Stern. He was a psychiatrist, a convert from Judaism to Catholicism, who expressed in a single paragraph of his autobiography,

The Pillar of Fire, words from a searching human heart, words that say what I am struggling to convey here in this four-sided consideration:

> I used to sit on a bench on Primrose Hill and look over all the City of London. If it were true, I used to think, that God had become man, and that his life and death had a personal meaning to every single person among all those millions of existences spent in the stench of slums, in a horizonless world, in the suffocating anguish of enmities, sickness and dying—if that were true, it would be something tremendously worth living for. To think that Someone knocked at all those millions of dark doors, beckoning and promising to each in an altogether unique way. Christ challenged not only the apparent chaos of history but the meaninglessness of personal existence.

The dimensions of Christmas stretch out first in a parallel movement of Trinitarian love, creating the human race. Then comes a vertical drop from grace, a free fall from that state of familiarity with God, from the condition of sharing the divine life and love. Next comes another vertical drop, a descent, the enfleshment of the eternal Word, who became the Word Incarnate so that God might move horizontally again, so to speak, among humankind, this time inviting a return to grace. The projected lines of redemption could not come together in closure, however, in this mysterious plan of God, without the death of the Word enfleshed and thus equipped with that "whereby he could die." After death, resurrection, and with it the possibility again of eternal life for Adam's race.

Christmas marked the "fullness of time" when God

saw fit to bridge the "chasm." God stepped into human history in a decisive, declarative, and salvific way to work the redemption of the human race. To cross from our side to his was beyond our power. To come from his side to ours was the original Christmas gift.

Each generation is born on our side of the chasm and is thus estranged and in need of salvation. This is true of every son and daughter of Adam; this is why innocent, helpless, beautiful infants—incapable of sinning on their own, but touched by the original sin of Adam and Eve—are brought to the baptismal font. Each Christmas celebration is a remembering that we were once lost, irreversibly so, from the standpoint of our ability to do anything about it, but now we are found.

If we believe in the Lordship of Christ and that the Father raised him from the dead, we too shall move through death to life. The Word moved from the everlasting to the transitory and back to the everlasting, and showed us the way.

> He is the image of the invisible God,
>   the firstborn of all creation.
> For in him were created all things
>   in heaven and on earth,
>   the visible and the invisible,
>   whether thrones or dominions
>   or principalities or powers;
>   all things were created through him
>   and for him.
> He is before all things,
>   and in him all things hold together.
> He is the head of the body, the church.
> He is the beginning,
>   the firstborn from the dead,

that in all things
he himself might be preeminent.
For in him
all the fullness was pleased to dwell,
and through him
to reconcile all things for him,
making peace by the blood of his cross...
(Col 1:15-20)

The path, the way God chose for himself and for us, in this transit through earthly life, has some hard conditions attached to it, as well as many joys. There is no escaping the fact that the peace embodied in the gift of Christ at Christmas has been sealed with the blood of his cross. In choosing to work it all out this way, God set a pattern. The outline of that pattern is repeated in the Acts of the Apostles (9:15), where the Lord, speaking of Paul, said to Ananias in a vision: "This man is a chosen instrument of mine to carry my name before Gentiles, kings, and Israelites, and I will show him what he will have to suffer for my name."

Every Christian is a "chosen instrument" of the Lord. In carrying his name as they make their way through the world, Christians "will have to suffer" to some extent, according to his plan.

The Christmas manger, straw, and midnight cold all serve to suggest that this pattern can be expected to be repeated, by God's will, in the life of every Christian. Accepting this fact in faith opens the Christian heart to the deepest possible Christmas peace.

Whether you kneel before the Christmas crib to ponder these mysteries, or walk outdoors in the imaginary footsteps of the shepherds, recalling what they saw and heard, or whether you gaze into the eyes of children and family on Christmas Day, all you can really say is what Augustine said centuries ago: "And now, with what words shall we praise the love of God? What thanks shall we give?"

EIGHT

Insights for a Christmas Meditation

No one I've read communicates both the profundity and the simplicity of the Christmas mystery more effectively than St. Augustine. Here are segments from his Christmas sermons. The insights are his; the opportunity to ponder them can be part of the Christmas celebration for anyone wise enough to want to take it. The selections are all taken from *Saint Augustine: Sermons for Christmas and Epiphany* (Newman Press, 1952).

In a beautiful expression of poetic wonder, Augustine says,

> When the Maker of time, the Word of the Father, was made flesh, He gave us His birthday in time; and He, without whose divine bidding no day runs its course, in His Incarnation reserved one day for Himself. He Himself with the Father precedes all spans of time; but on this day, issuing from His mother, He stepped into the tide of the years.
>
> Man's Maker was made man, that He, Ruler of the stars, might nurse at His mother's breasts; that the Bread might be hungry, the Fountain thirst, the Light sleep, the Way be tired from the journey; that the Truth might be accused by false

witnesses, the Judge of the living and the dead be judged by a mortal judge, Justice be sentenced by the unjust, the Teacher be beaten with whips, the Vine be crowned with thorns, the Foundation be suspended on wood; that Strength might be made weak, that He who makes well might be wounded, that Life might die. He was made man to suffer these and similar undeserved things for us, that He might free us who were undeserving; and He who on account of us endured such great evils, merited no evil, while we, who through Him were so bountifully blessed, had no merits to show for such blessings. (Sermon No. 9)

From the depths of what can only be called contemplative wonder, Augustine again exclaims:

And now, with what words shall we praise the love of God? What thanks shall we give? He so loved us that for our sakes He, through whom time was made, was made in time; and He, older by eternity than the world itself, was younger in age than many of His servants in the world; He, who made man, was made man; He was given existence by a mother whom He brought into existence; He was carried in hands that He formed; He was nursed at breasts that He filled; He cried like a babe in the manger in speechless infancy—this Word without which human eloquence is speechless. (Sermon No. 6)

Augustine repeatedly refers to the twofold birth of Christ, one in eternity, and the other in time. Borrowing language from the psalms, he writes:

We are not yet able to contemplate the fact that He was begotten by the Father before the Daystar; but let us keep in our thoughts the fact that He was born of a virgin during the hours of night. (Sermon No. 12)

The two-birth theme touches the pivotal question of whether Jesus of Nazareth was God incarnate—the question of the divinity of Christ. This was an issue with which Augustine had to deal in the fourth-century controversy over Arianism, a heresy that denied the divinity of Christ.

With our Catholic faith we ought to hold fast that the Lord has two births, the one divine, the other human; the one timeless and the other in time. Both moreover are extraordinary: the one without a mother, the other without a father. (Sermon No. 3)

What, then, does the Catholic faith say? The Son is God of God the Father; God the Father is God, but not of the Son. At the same time God the Son is equal with the Father—born equal, not born less; not made equal, but born equal. What the one is, the other who was born is also. (Sermon No. 15)

Let no one, therefore, believe that the Son of God was changed or transformed into the Son of man; but rather let us believe that He, remaining the Son of God, was made the Son of man, without loss of His divine substance and by a perfect assumption of the human substance. (Sermon No. 5)

In fact, Christ was born both of a father and of a
mother, both without a father and without a
mother; of a father as God, of a mother as man;
without a mother as God, without a father as
man. (Sermon No. 2)

Another theme that fascinated Augustine was that of
the Virgin Birth. He offers examples of actions performed
by the man Christ, in displays of divine power, to explain
the miraculous circumstances of His birth in time.

And despite the mass of His body, a body in the
flower of manhood, He entered in where His disci-
ples were behind locked doors. Why, then, if in
adult age He was able to enter through closed
doors, should He not have been able as an infant
to issue from His mother and leave her members
unimpaired? But the unbelieving will not believe
the one thing or the other.... This is precisely
what constitutes unbelief, that Christ is held to be
without any divinity whatsoever. (Sermon No. 9)

Why do you marvel? He is God. Consider His
divinity, and the cause of your marvelling vanishes. And when we say, "He was born of a virgin," this is something extraordinary—you marvel.
He is God; you must not marvel. Let our surprise
yield to thanksgiving. Have faith; believe for this
really so happened. (Sermon No. 7)

...[A] virgin before marriage, a virgin in marriage—a virgin with Child, a virgin nursing the
Child! For indeed, when her Omnipotent Son was
born, He in no manner at all took away the vir-

ginity of His holy mother whom He had chosen
when He was to be born. (Sermon No. 6)

In Augustine's view the virgins of Christ—those who
choose virginity for the sake of the kingdom—have first
claim to the joy of Christmas morning because "the Mother
of God is one of you." (Sermon No. 10)

> She, then, whose footsteps you follow, not only
> did not cohabit with a man that she might con-
> ceive, but in giving birth remained a virgin.
> Imitate her to the best of your ability....And you
> must not think of yourselves as sterile merely
> because you remain virgins. For it is precisely this
> holy purity of the flesh that also leads to fruitful-
> ness of the spirit....that you may have, not a
> womb fruitful with offspring, but a spirit fruitful
> with virtues. (Sermon No. 9)

St. Augustine liked to refer to Christ as the "Bridegroom" who came forth from the bridal chamber—the
Virgin's womb—"where the Word of God was united to
human creation." Christ, of course, is the bridegroom of the
Church, and the Church, for its part, is virgin and mother.
How the Church has perpetual virginity and inviolate fecun-
dity is explained by Augustine in these words:

> Why should not you [the people] be concerned in
> the Virgin's childbearing, seeing that you are the
> members of Christ? Mary gave birth to your Head;
> the Church gave birth to you. For the Church her-
> self is also mother and virgin: a mother through
> loving charity, a virgin through the soundness of
> her faith and sanctity. She gives birth to peoples,
> but her members belong to the One only of whom

she herself is the body and spouse. In this, too, she bears the likeness of that other Virgin, the fact that she is also the mother of unity among men. (Sermon No. 10)

Whether you kneel before the Christmas crib to ponder these mysteries, or walk outdoors in the imaginary footsteps of the shepherds, recalling what they saw and heard, or whether you gaze into the eyes of children and family on Christmas Day, all you can really say is what Augustine said centuries ago: "And now, with what words shall we praise the love of God? What thanks shall we give?"

It is "by invitation only" that you relate to God. The invitation comes in a "whisper," an inner impulse, a certain sense within you of "being-inclined-to," or being drawn toward God. There are no flashes of light; no bells go off. No special "appearances." There is nothing resembling what the religious lexicon would call an "apparition." No, just a whisper. That's normally all you'll get; and that is all you need. But the whisper is an invitation. You have to R.S.V.P.

NINE

Listen to the Whispers

For many years I've appreciated the special applicability to Christmas of a thought expressed by Edward Schillebeeckx, O.P., in *Christ the Sacrament of Encounter with God:* "It [the world and life in the world] interprets dimly at least something of that which God personally, by the attraction of his grace, is whispering in our hearts." Our task, as Christians, I've often thought, is to improve the environment within which that whisper can be heard. The "acoustics" need improvement and they should improve, it seems to me, whenever and wherever Christian faith meets daily life in secular surroundings.

Christ broke into the awareness of the world, like a whisper, in the event we celebrate at Christmas. He came in an attractive way. The mission begun at Bethlehem works by attraction. The human response to Christ is voluntary, non-coercive. It works only by attraction, hence the importance of the whispers of grace in an atmosphere of faith.

The lives and works of Christians interpret "dimly at least something of that which God personally, by the attraction of his grace, is whispering" in our world today. The Christian should be alert, of course, to what those whispers may be saying to himself or herself. The Christmas holidays are busy, but not so busy that they cannot provide, for those who want to take it, some "downtime" to attend to the whisper in their own hearts, the whisper from the God who is always at work in the world on each of the 365 days of Christmas and who never stops calling each one of us in an altogether unique way. It is unique because there is a person-to-Person relationship of grace between you and your creating-sustaining Lord.

It is "by invitation only" that you relate to God. The invitation comes in a "whisper," an inner impulse, a certain sense within you of "being-inclined-to," or being drawn toward God. There are no flashes of light; no bells go off. No special "appearances." There is nothing resembling what the religious lexicon would call an "apparition." No, just a whisper. That's normally all you'll get; and that is all you need. But the whisper is an invitation. You have to R.S.V.P.

An invitation, you should not fail to notice, is an affirmation of your person: *you* are invited; the pleasure of *your* company is requested. An invitation is not a command; it respects your freedom. When God, who is always asking and bidding, calls you, it is often in the circumstances of your life and in words spoken by human voices. Not every voice, however, speaks for God to you. It is your job to sift out the voices and sort out the circumstances. You don't have to. Being free means you are free to miss the call. That's the point of that very sad verse in the prologue of the gospel of John: "To his very own he came, yet his own did not accept him."

Christmas provides not only the time to listen to "the whisper," to do the sifting and sorting out of the "messages" that life delivers every day; it also offers a model in the person of the carpenter Joseph, a model for the necessary discernment. Yes, I know, the gospel story says an angel came to him in a dream and gave him a "command." "Joseph, son of David, do not be afraid to take Mary home as your wife...." The story, as Matthew (1:18-24) recounts it, is, of course, the Christmas story:

> Now this is how the birth of Jesus Christ came about. When his mother Mary was betrothed to Joseph, but before they lived together, she was found with child through the Holy Spirit. Joseph her husband, since he was a righteous man, yet unwilling to expose her to shame, decided to divorce her quietly. Such was his intention when, behold, the angel of the Lord appeared to him in a dream and said, "Joseph, son of David, do not be afraid to take Mary your wife into your home. For it is through the Holy Spirit that this child has been conceived in her. She will bear a son and you are to name him Jesus, because he will save his people from their sins." All this took place to fulfill what the Lord had said through the prophet:
>
> > "Behold, the virgin shall be with child
> > and bear a son,
> > and they shall call him Emmanuel,"
>
> which means "God is with us." When Joseph awoke, he did as the angel of the Lord had commanded him and took his wife into his home.

No small fix for Joseph to find himself in. He had already made up his mind. His intention was set—until the message got through. The law told him that Mary had to be set aside, cut off, and the engagement broken. But love prompted Joseph to want to spare her any pain and publicity. And an even deeper love prompted him to take God's message and messenger seriously, although it was all in a dream. How could he, like anyone else, know for sure where dreams end and reality begins. Still, he decided to trust God and set up a household with Mary, even though he could not unravel the mystery surrounding her.

What if Joseph had done what the law required, once he learned that Mary was with child? Fortunately for him, and us, and the entire human race, he decided that the ultimate law was the will of God that could be made known to him in a dream, or a whisper, or in an inner conviction that this, and not that, was the right thing to do.

There is one last point of the Christmas proclamation that can only be communicated in a whisper. Commercialism and consumerism will shout down any suggestion that Christmas has anything to do with poverty. We believers have to encourage one another with whispered reminders that the divine life became incarnate *as poor.* The poverty to note is not what you might first suspect. It is not as not having, that divine life entered our world. Rather, it is a poverty of *having given* and of continually giving of what one has and who one is. He "emptied himself," Paul tells the Philippians in describing the "attitude" of the Son who chose not to "cling" to his divinity in a way that would hold him back from entering fully into the human condition.

Your Christmas consideration of his example will raise the question of to what extent your life, in imitation of the poor Christ, is a life of generosity—of giving and giving more of what you have and who you are. It would be wonderful if you could look at the Christmas gifts you give as simple signs of this deeper reality. It would be equally wonderful if you could look at the Christmas gifts you receive as windows on the goodness and generosity of the givers. Most wonderful of all, however, would be your ability to see Christ in all the gifts. Then you might be ready to hear a whispered suggestion that a poverty of spirit—a certain detachment from material things, a condition of being fixed in the things of eternity so that you can sit loose to the things of time—is the only way to make room for the God who wants to dwell within you and bring you lasting peace.

It is easy to indulge, even overindulge in the beauty of Christmas—the lights, the music, the gifts, the warmth of human love; the food, and drink, and decorations; the coming together of families. You can and should enjoy all the beautiful elements of Christmas and give thanks to God for the happiness they bring. But they will move you forward on the path that leads to everlasting life only to the extent that they serve to deepen your faith in the mystery of the cross—the cross in the life of Christ, of course, but also and inevitably in the life of every Christian.

TEN

Two Sides of Christmas—The Severe and the Beautiful

According to Cardinal John Henry Newman, "religion has two sides, a severe side, and a beautiful; and we shall be sure to swerve from the narrow way which leads to life, if we indulge ourselves in what is beautiful while we put aside what is severe."

Christmas also has two sides—the severe and the beautiful. And Christians can easily swerve from what Newman calls "the narrow way which leads to life" if they over-indulge in the beautiful while ignoring the severe.

A Christmas card I received years ago put the issue plainly in artwork that juxtaposed the Christmas Crib with the Cross of Calvary. Beneath the two were the following words from the fourth gospel: "For this I was born, for this I came into the world..." (Jn 18:37), words spoken by Jesus late in his public life in response to Pilate's question, "Then you are a king?" From the "this" of the manger to the "this" of the crucifixion you have the full explanation of the meaning of the life of the anointed one, the Christ, whose birth is the focus of the Christmas celebration. From the wood of the crib to the wood of the cross: this summarizes the life that began for Christ in Bethlehem, and traces "the narrow way which leads to life" for every Christian.

There is exquisite beauty in Christmas, but severity as well. "While they were there (in Bethlehem), the time came for her to have her child, and she gave birth to her firstborn son. She wrapped him in swaddling clothes and laid him in a manger, because there was no room for them in the inn" (Lk 2:6-7). A beautiful scene.

That scene, made attractive by Christmas art, is based on the severe, even harsh reality of homelessness. No linen, no satin, no sanitation. But so much love, so much faith, so much commitment; the beauty of these realities transcends the severity of the immediate surroundings. The same beauty and the same realities—love, faith, commitment—bring the same transcending power into the life of every Christian, of every Joseph and Mary, of every person whose life is grounded in and turned around by him whose life on earth had such austere beginnings.

It is easy to indulge, even overindulge in the beauty of Christmas—the lights, the music, the gifts, the warmth of human love; the food, and drink, and decorations; the coming together of families. You can and should enjoy all the beautiful elements of Christmas and give thanks to God for the happiness they bring. But they will move you forward on the path that leads to everlasting life only to the extent that they serve to deepen your faith in the mystery of the cross—the cross in the life of Christ, of course, but also and inevitably in the life of every Christian.

Death can and often does come during the Christmas holidays. Mourning seems all the more awkward and heavy then. Illness is always a part of the human condition; it doesn't go away at Christmastime. Disappointments, misunderstandings, failures of one kind or another, can all coexist with the Christmas celebration. The eye of Christian and Christmas faith sees salvation in the link between the crib and the cross. The child adored in the manger will later die and rise for your redemption. You will rise as he did, you know that in faith; and you have that knowledge as part of the promise of Christmas.

You will rise from death, even though your death is not likely to approach the severity of his. Whenever, wherever, however you die, the promise of Christmas says you are going to rise again.

You will also rise from this life's disappointments and failures if you simply entrust yourself to this Christ who came to give meaning to this life. You will rise above your selfishness, your pettiness, your jealousy, and even your tendency now and then to hate, if you permit yourself to be moved by the power of this Christmas mystery, this Christmas gift from God to you, the gift of salvation in Christ.

Christmas is the time to open up your heart in gratitude—not just vertically upward, so to speak, in thanks to God, but horizontally outward toward your brothers and sisters in the human community as your gratitude to God above finds expression in love for those around you. Love of neighbor is powerful enough to sweep away the pettiness, the envy, and the hatred that can kill the Christmas spirit and your happiness along with it.

Christmas, like religion, "has two sides, a severe side, and a beautiful; and we shall be sure to swerve from the narrow way which leads to life, if we indulge ourselves in what is beautiful while we put aside what is severe," to quote once again the wise words of Cardinal Newman. They invite you to locate yourself between the crib and the cross where God located himself before you.

The all-powerful One chose helpless, dependent infancy for a purpose. Immensity chose to accept limits; the unknowable chose to become known; the unapproachable chose to become an infant anyone could approach, and touch, and love. The immutable God was moved with pity and chose to suffer—for a purpose. And the purpose, of course, was your salvation.

In Christ, in Christmas, in the span between crib and cross, you can find an explanation of yourself. You can find meaning for your life. You can find purpose, and peace, and the joy the triune God intended to be your gift, in Christ, at Christmas.

With the brush of affluence, we seem to have painted ourselves, as family members and as members of the larger society, into a very private but deeply lonely corner. How do we get out of that corner? The only way out is by coming together.

ELEVEN

Family

The famous opening sentence in Tolstoy's *Anna Karenina* always runs through my mind at Christmastime: "All happy families are alike but an unhappy family is unhappy after its own fashion." Christmas is as close as we ever come to having all families happy. Why are highways, air and rail terminals jammed at that time of year? Where is everyone going? Home to family and friends, for the most part; or off for a holiday break after spending some time with family and friends. Generous and thoughtful efforts bordering on rescue operations take place in every community to "make sure" isolated, unrelated persons living alone have "a place to go" for Christmas dinner. The place to go is family, someone's family at any rate. Those fond of compiling "happiness is" lists, would surely agree that "sadness is" dining alone on Christmas Day.

Unhappy families, each after its own fashion, are part of the Christmas reality. The day ends badly in many households. The probability of change or improvement in the New Year is often not high.

The Church speaks to families—happy and unhappy—on the Sunday between Christmas and New Year's Day. It is Holy Family Sunday honoring Jesus, Mary, and Joseph as a family unit worthy of imitation. Familiar scripture readings of enduring beauty are proclaimed again each year, then extended into homilies, and listened to in faith. The readings do not change, but the social forces surrounding family life do change, so much so that it becomes necessary, for the good of family and society alike, to bring faith and family together for reflective purposes in the Christmas season.

This means returning to the fundamental meaning of family, the social unit that draws life from the love of a man for a woman and a woman for a man, a social unit that fosters the attitudes of care and concern, where mature adults are called to a vocation of service to life, and to live that vocation by laying down their lives, day by day, for one another and for the children their love brings forth.

It is a commonplace that cannot be repeated too often that the family is the cornerstone of society. It is our fundamental, foundational social unit. Where family life is in trouble, society is also in trouble, deep trouble.

Many of the troubles in contemporary American society derive directly from troubles in American family life. And where something goes deeply and disastrously wrong in the family, it is usually because members of the family refuse to measure up to the demands of sacrifice.

The word "sacrifice" means to make holy. No family can be a "holy family" without sacrifice. And no family can be a happy family unless it rests on holiness—not pietistic, multiple-devotion "holiness," but genuine holiness—sacrifice that requires the gift of self to and for others.

In the days before the Catholic Mass changed from Latin to the vernacular languages, the Wedding Mass in the United States began with an English "exhortation" read by the priest to the couple about to exchange their vows. It contained a great deal of wisdom capable of holding families and societies together. The heart of that exhortation is expressed in these few words: "Let the security of your wedded life rest on the great principle of self-sacrifice. Sacrifice is usually difficult and irksome; only love can make it easy, and perfect love can make it a joy." Love, in the wisdom-vocabulary of the Church, is another word for sacrifice.

The absence of sacrifice in our homes and in our nation explains, to no small extent, the absence of familial and national happiness. Something happened to America after the Second World War. "Affluence" is one way to describe it. Our present national discontent and insecurity invite us to face up to the fact that sparing and sharing will be more beneficial than the unimpeded consumerism and waste to which we've grown accustomed.

In our families, we see higher divorce rates, deeper loneliness, and much alienation; this is evidence that the self-sacrifice upon which the security and happiness of family life depend have all but vanished from our midst. Only persons, particularly persons in families, can choose to restore it. Pressured, perhaps, by environmental concerns or the promptings of social justice, we can as a nation decide to become a bit more sparing and sharing. We can also choose to react to the increased pressures on family stability by caring more for others and less for self. This will strengthen the family unit, and that, of course, means a strengthening of the larger society.

Affluence has had an atomizing and privatizing impact on contemporary American family life. Material progress has produced so many "private and personal" things—cars, rooms, phones, radios, television sets, stereos, and all the other hardware and software that make us less dependent on one another, but isolate us from close, physical, tangible contact at home, while enabling our isolated selves to reach out and electronically "touch" someone anywhere in the world.

With the brush of affluence, we seem to have painted

ourselves, as family members and as members of the larger society, into a very private but deeply lonely corner. How do we get out of that corner? The only way out is by coming together. One of the scripture readings the Church offers for consideration on Holy Family Sunday holds an exit route from the self-enclosure that sometimes sets family members apart from one another:

> Put on then, as God's chosen ones, holy and beloved, heartfelt compassion, kindness, humility, gentleness and patience, bearing with one another and forgiving one another, if one has a grievance against another; as the Lord has forgiven you, so must you also do (Col 3:12-13).

Forgiveness is the key. It has to be spoken, and when it is spoken at Christmas time, it translates advice from the Book of Sirach into a principle of family reinforcement: "Sometimes the word means more than the gift" (Sir 18:16). Forgiveness can heal family wounds, tighten up family structures. Forgiveness means giving and restoring, reinstating and forgetting, when restoration and reinstatement are not deserved. The Letter to the Colossians calls us to forgive as the Lord has forgiven us. Who among us deserved the gift God gave us in Christ? Remember, "A gift is when you get something you don't deserve." Who can say he or she deserved the reconciliation with the Father achieved in the broken body of Christ. No one of us had any title at all to reinstatement in the life of grace, no claim to the forgiveness we have all received.

Aware of having been forgiven and yet still needing forgiveness in Jesus Christ, believers should extend to each other forgiveness now and the promise of future forgiveness. That, of course, is what it means to forgive as the

Lord has forgiven you. Yet, how unlike the Lord are so many members of so many families in the matter of forgiveness. How many of us say we forgive and stoutly refuse to forget, or let others forget? Who ever heard of forgiving a debt by requiring payment in full? And yet you can't help noticing, when families get together, how some members exact painfully full payment by inflicting sharp words or long silences, deep hurts and stinging sarcasm on other members of the family. Sometimes this is preamble to the conferral, with great reluctance and no small righteousness, of my forgiveness. "As the Lord has forgiven you, you must also do."

Holy Family Sunday is as good a day as any, and better than most, to consider that God might be inviting you to walk on the path of forgiveness toward other members of your family from whom you may have separated yourself, if not spatially perhaps emotionally, psychologically, or spiritually. This could be healing time. With the healing comes a stronger family unit, and with that a stronger and better society.

I know this sounds idealistic and I realize that division and differences are part of any family life. Henri de Lubac's words have always made a lot of sense to me: "To differ, even deeply, from one another is not to be enemies; it is simply to be. To recognize and accept one's own difference is not pride. To recognize and accept the difference of others is not weakness. If union has to be, if union offers any meaning at all, it must be union between different people. And it is above all in the recognition and acceptance of difference that difference is overcome and union achieved." That, as I indicated, makes a lot of sense to me.

Another comment along these lines that makes a good deal of sense is Sam Rayburn's observation that "when two people always agree about everything, it just goes to prove that one of them is doing all the thinking."

All happy families are alike in this regard, and happy families have differences that are not necessarily divisive and certainly not destructive. I'd find it reassuring, however, if more families would adopt those words I've already quoted from the Letter to the Colossians as kind of a family creed, or charter, or collective agenda. But what I quoted above is not the complete text used on Holy Family Sunday. It is important to complete the quotation: "And over all these put on love, that is, the bond of perfection. And let the peace of Christ control your hearts, the peace into which you were also called in one body. And be thankful. Let the word of Christ dwell in you richly, as in all wisdom you teach and admonish one another, singing psalms, hymns, and spiritual songs with gratitude in your hearts to God. And whatever you do, in word or in deed, do everything in the name of the Lord Jesus, giving thanks to God the Father through him" (Col 3:14-17).

Even though Mary was destined from the moment of her conception to become God's mother, it is altogether possible for today's young women to relate to her. She was gifted with freedom from Original Sin, but not from the problems of physical and psychological development, from doubt and disappointment, and from all the other uncertainties of life. Today's adolescent girl and Mary have a lot in common.

TWELVE

Mary and the Other Madonna

It would be wonderful if, by the time these words find their way into print, references to "the other Madonna" would draw expressions of puzzled unknowing. Forgotten, but not yet gone, would, in my view, be the ideal consignment into oblivion for the entertainer, "The Material Girl," who became in the 1980s the heroine and role model of millions of teenagers around the world.

Mary, the Mother of God, was a teenager, an adolescent, an inhabitant of that territory west of childhood known as the early teen years. Any female who inhabits that same territory now, or remembers being there, can identify with Mary. She was, of course, the Mother of God, the wife of Joseph, the mother of Jesus; she was indeed the Madonna. She was at the same time a teenager—not just like, but enough like any teenage girl you've ever known.

A study commissioned by the Carnegie Council on Adolescent Development is titled "At the Threshold: The Developing Adolescent." Mary was, of course, "at the threshold" when the angel informed her that she was to be the Mother of God. She was a "developing adolescent" when she was faced with the choice made famous for all time by her response: "May it be done to me according to your word" (Lk 1:38). With Mary in mind, consider the findings of the Carnegie report.

In undertaking this study, the research group was charged "to focus on normal development among early and middle adolescents, to review the biological, cognitive, and social factors that, in combination, influence the course of adolescent development...."

Think of what would presumably have been normal development for Mary during early and middle adolescence. What is known of adolescent development today would be generally applicable to her. Think of what the researchers call "the biological, cognitive, and social factors that, in combination, influence the course of adolescent development." With obvious allowances for twenty centuries of human progress, you still have rough reference points to help you locate, on a developmental scale, the young girl who carried a mysterious pregnancy to term in the circumstances we recall in the Christmas commemoration. Even though Mary was destined from the moment of her conception to become God's mother, it is altogether possible for today's young women to relate to her. She was gifted with freedom from Original Sin, but not from the problems of physical and psychological development, from doubt and disappointment, and from all the other uncertainties of life. Today's adolescent girl and Mary have a lot in common.

Normal teenagers participate in a search for self: who am I? what am I going to be, to become? Mary's shock when the Angel Gabriel appeared to her indicates that she had no previous knowledge of where her life was going. In that respect, she was a normal adolescent.

Teenagers typically experiment with various personae, imagining themselves to be this person or that, preoccupied with the challenge of self-definition. The Carnegie researchers report that the outcome of the adolescent's experimental search for self-definition "can profoundly influence the future." That was surely true in Mary's case. Here's what the researchers, not, of course, with Mary in mind, have to say: "Evidence reveals that, among early adolescents, the cognitive shifts from concrete thought to abstract reasoning [schools provide algebra to facilitate that shift] is accompanied by a shift from concrete self-definition to more abstract self-portraiture that describes their psychological interior. As they become more aware of their different 'selves,' many teenagers become troubled by the inconsistencies. Older adolescents, once they have traversed this difficult stage, no longer experience such internal conflict."

Twelve-year-olds may see nothing inconsistent in a decision to be nice to friends and mean to people who don't treat them well. The older adolescent sees something wrong with that and is troubled when his or her behavior reveals that inconsistency. "That's not the real me; I don't want to say what I just said." Or it may play out this way: "I let myself get depressed, and I know I want to be happy, but I won't let others know how much I really want to be happy. I want them to think I like being miserable." It is curious, but not surprising to note, as many teenagers and their families know, that this can happen at Christmas time.

The Carnegie study relates that adolescents live much of their lives performing before what the researchers call the "imaginary audience." Youngsters falsely assume that others are as preoccupied with their behavior and appearance as they are. As one teenager put it: "Everybody, I mean everybody, else is looking at me like they think I'm totally weird."

Well, I am not about to suggest that Mary saw things exactly this way, but she certainly had to wonder what others thought of her, and she surely was not insensitive to the opinions of others. I'm sure she wanted to be liked. She was a normal teenager.

Central to normal adolescent development and happy teenage living is the concept of self-esteem. The Carnegie researchers identify five areas where, in the opinion of today's adolescents, success is necessary in order to enjoy self-esteem. Here, in the order of importance—as teenagers rank them—are the key areas: (1) appearance, (2) scholastic competence, (3) social acceptance, (4) athletic competence, and (5) behavioral conduct.

It is easy to see how stress can develop in a teenager's life as he or she tries to attain some measure of success in all or most of these categories. Role models enter the picture here—athletes, entertainers, academic achievers, good-looking, poised, "cool," "with-it" upperclassmen. And along comes Madonna, quite literally waiting in the wings, to show the adolescent girl how she really ought to live her life. That, at least, is what millions of adolescent girls have been willing to let her do.

A serious pre-Christmas opinion piece in *The New York Times* asserted: "Madonna is the true feminist. She exposes the puritanism and suffocating ideology of American feminism, which is stuck in an adolescent whining mode. Madonna has taught young women to be fully female and sexual while still exercising total control over their lives. She shows girls how to be attractive, sensual, energetic, ambitious, aggressive and funny—all at the same time" (Camille Paglia, "Madonna—Finally, a Real Feminist").

Imitating Madonna is one way to react to the stress generated by failure to make high marks in one or more of those five areas of success America's adolescents identified as most important in enabling them to grow in self-esteem: appearance, scholastic competence, social acceptance, athletic competence, and behavioral conduct. Imitating Mary is a better way.

Even the Carnegie study says that "research on personality characteristics indicates that being sensitive, cooperative, socially responsible, emotionally stable, and active can help youngsters do well under adverse life conditions." Mary did very well under extraordinarily adverse life conditions of poverty, hopelessness, confusion about identity, and uncertainty about the future. Who was ever more "sensitive, cooperative, socially responsible, emotionally stable, and active" than she? And her greatest virtue—faith—makes her most imitable for anyone willing to take the leap, as she did, of trusting God absolutely and unconditionally. "May it be done to me according to your word." Anyone willing to entrust oneself completely and entirely to the providence of God is capable of imitating Mary the Mother of God. Any Christian unwilling to do that is missing the meaning of Christmas.

The Carnegie study identifies "two fundamentally different responses to difficulty or challenge" as found in the behavior patterns of middle childhood. One is a "mastery-oriented" response. The other is a "helpless" response. Developing youngsters carry those response tendencies with them from middle childhood into the teen years; sometimes the "helpless" response continues on into adulthood. That was not the case with Mary then, nor, from all appearances, with Madonna now. But Mary's "mastery-oriented response" did not take the materialism route that Madonna's celebrated value system promotes.

The Carnegie researchers have more to say on these two response mechanisms youngsters tend to use when the going gets rough:

In the helpless pattern, children seem trapped by

the experience of difficulty, attributing it to a lack of ability. They often say things like, 'I'm not smart at this,' even when they have demonstrated their ability in many similar situations. They feel anxious and upset about difficulty. Under pressure, or in the face of failure, they may lapse into less sophisticated problem-solving strategies, slackening their effort as well as losing sight of task objectives. These children seem to believe that intelligence is something that they cannot change and that the failure is an indictment of their ability.

Mastery-oriented children, in contrast, remain extremely dedicated to the task, despite difficulty. They seem to believe that they can become more intelligent through effort. These children use effective problem-solving strategies, like structuring themselves to think carefully, to pay attention, and to remember. They report feeling excited and spurred by difficulty rather than threatened or anxious....

These patterns describe many adolescents' reactions to the challenges, obstacles, and setbacks they may encounter in domains other than education—in sports, social life, and work.

It is worth a moment's thought at Christmastime to wonder whether adolescent girls and young women in contemporary America will choose, not simply between the "helpless" response and the "mastery-oriented" approach to life's difficulties, but whether they will go the route of Mary's mastery-oriented response, or choose Madonna's mastery-style as a pattern for their lives.

The familiar Christmas gospel tells the story of a fifteen- or sixteen-year-old named Mary, who traveled up from Nazareth to Judea to the town of Bethlehem. And while there, as every believer knows, "the time came for her to have her child, and she gave birth to her firstborn son. She wrapped him in swaddling clothes and laid him in a manger because there was no room for them in the inn" (Lk 2:6–7). She is universally revered as the Blessed Mother. But, in age and appearance, she was not like the mothers most teenagers know as their own. She was herself a teenager, who put herself in God's hands and believed, and trusted, and responded with resourcefulness and generous self-donation to the needs of another who was the helpless infant God entrusted to her care.

It is clear that Mary was more concerned about meeting the needs of others than with having her own needs met. She was preoccupied with another, not herself. She was "sensitive, cooperative, socially responsible, emotionally stable, and active"—all those things that the Carnegie researchers say are important to "help youngsters do well under adverse life conditions." Youngsters like this, the report says, "tend to be self-confident and have high self-esteem; they have feelings of personal power." All of that is a description of Mary. She had all the things today's teenagers are searching for. What a pity that so many teenagers turn to the other Madonna, not to Mary, for travel advice on the road to fulfillment. Looking to the wrong person, they get the wrong directions, and come up empty in their quest for happiness.

Barbara Boggs Sigmund—wife, mother, writer, poet, and innovative mayor of Princeton, New Jersey, until she died of cancer in 1990—wrote a 1987 essay calling upon the Pope to "bring back Mary" to Catholic devotional life. "Modern women in particular need her," wrote Mrs. Sigmund, to validate female strength-in-gentleness in the world of power. We are entering that world inexorably but uncertainly, jealous of both our femininity and our detachment. We resist taking on the 'pinstripes of the oppressor,' but all of our archetypes of power are male ones: the warrior, the team, the old bulls and the young. We need a model of our own on the grand scale.

So bring back Mary...to celebrate the need for the tough tenderness of femaleness in the life of the world, to acknowledge that charm and kindness can still entice God to dwell among us.

Now there's something all of us—male and female, old and young, but especially those who are both young and female—to think about as we shuffle our Christmas cards and count our Christmas blessings.

In some strange way, time stops—momentarily, at least—for the believer on Christmas night. In the stillness, however fleeting, for those who experience it, there is a special moment. In the framework of faith, it can all come together in a moment of recognition: sin meant separation; salvation means a return to grace, and Christmas brings that to you, personally, as gift—pure, unmerited, undeserved gift.

THIRTEEN

"Cast Out Our Sin and Enter In..."

Mentioned in a verse of the Christmas carol that keeps the "Little Town of Bethlehem" alive in Christian hearts and memory, "sin" doesn't sound so bad. In Christmas song, it is not a harsh word. It is simply that from which the Savior saves. It was spoken of by the prophets and laid out clearly at the beginning of the gospel story, "You are to name him Jesus because he will save his people from their sins" (Mt 1:21).

There you have the most basic reason for Christmas joy. To savor that joy fully, it helps to appreciate the meaning of the name Jesus: "Yahweh saves"—the Lord (Je) is our salvation (sus). Salvation from what? Sin, of course. But what is sin?

Sin is selfishness in the extreme. It is self-enclosure, preoccupation with self. Sin is a refusal to love, to love God or other persons in the human community. Sin is self-will to the point of rejecting God's will; it is a choice of darkness over light. It is willfully to harm another, willfully to break important promises, to walk over the lives and feelings of others, to ignore the needs of others, to prefer self to others, even God. Sin is separation from God. Christmas says you have been saved from the consequences of all that!

You can get a better idea of what sin is if you imagine

your union with God to be like a marriage bond, a covenant, a sacred and solemn commitment. Just as a husband or wife can break the marriage vow and seek union with another, so you can turn away from God. That's sin. Adam did just that. You inherited the effects of his "original" sin, and once you became mature, you learned the hard way that you yourself can sin.

Christmas invites you to climb out of your sinful self for a moment, to recognize your undeservedness and celebrate your salvation.

In some strange way, time stops—momentarily, at least—for the believer on Christmas night. In the stillness, however fleeting, for those who experience it, there is a special moment. In the framework of faith, it can all come together in a moment of recognition: sin meant separation; salvation means a return to grace, and Christmas brings that to you, personally, as gift—pure, unmerited, undeserved gift. You are gifted. Because of the Christmas event, because of what began on earth in that little town of Bethlehem, God entered into your history and cast out your sin. Pure gift. And this gift quite literally keeps on giving all year long.

I have no sure knowledge of when and how gift-giving became part of the Christmas celebration for families and friends. But I would hope the custom could be put to work to reinforce the sense of giftedness, undeserved giftedness, that is ours in Christ. We celebrate God's gift to us by giving gifts to one another at Christmastime. Theoretically, at least, that's the way it should be. But, O Lord—or, as one Christmas commentator put it, "Oh, Lord & Taylor!"—how far removed from the deep and simple meaning of Christmas has Christmas gift-giving become in modern times. And, sad to say, how evident is our present sinfulness, our preoccupation with self, in the ambiguity that surrounds the curious calculus of our own giving and receiving of Christmas gifts.

We *say* it is the thought that counts, but we act—in giving and receiving—as if the dollar price of what we give or receive is what *really* counts.

The famous writer of short fiction, O. Henry, created a beautiful Christmas story known to just about everyone. "The Gift of the Magi" finds the young wife Della frantic and depressed at Christmas because she has just a dollar or two to use to buy a gift for her husband Jim, who is also financially strapped and saddened because he cannot afford an expensive gift for her.

Della has long, beautiful hair and decides to sell it to get enough money to buy for Jim a platinum fob chain to adorn his one prize possession, a handsome gold pocket-watch that belonged to his father and grandfather before him. And Jim, as those who know the story will recall, decides on Christmas Eve to sell the watch in order to be able to buy an expensive set of pure tortoise-shell combs, with jeweled rims, to give to Della to adorn her beautiful hair.

When they exchanged their gifts on Christmas Eve—beautiful combs for her who had sold her hair; a handsome watch-fob for him who had pawned his watch—they suddenly realized that the gifts were unimportant. The only thing of any consequence was their love for one another.

"And you are to name him Jesus because he will save his people from their sins." God's gift of love to us at Christmas came wrapped, quite literally, in "swaddling clothes" and packaged in straw. Our love for one another is the gift that carries the meaning of Christmas. The eye of the imagination can "see" Christmas love in the smiling faces of Della and Jim, whose transparent emptying out of self, one for the other, made their Christmas Day. Moments like that can happen any day between selfless people. And Christmas could be everyday, everywhere, if people would live out the implications of the recognition of their unde-servedness in the face of God's gift to them of life, and love, and grace—everything that came to us when God "saved his people from their sins."

Regrettably, the meaning of our Christmas giftedness has been ground under by our measured practice of Christmas gift-giving. Forgetting our undeservedness, we permit the exchange of expensive things to heighten those materialistic instincts that encourage us to live as if there were no God, no sin, no need for salvation. We become trapped in the ambiguity of the season and forget the profound reality behind the angel's instruction to Joseph: "She is to have a son, and you are to name him Jesus because he will save his people from their sins."

As Christmas turns into Epiphany, and Epiphany reopens the door to "ordinary time" and ordinary life, you can consider anew your opportunity to be a saint, to let that little light of yours shine and brighten your corner of a troubled world.

FOURTEEN

Epiphany

Epiphany marks the end of the Christmas season and the beginning of a renewed effort to "show forth," for all the world to notice, what it means to be a Christian.

"In times of extreme social and political distress, God is hidden; and it is the saint who makes God reappear," writes theologian Lawrence Cunningham in an essay on the saints. Some might want to argue that God is even less noticeable in times of prosperity. People enjoying security and affluence are all too easily distracted from God. They are less likely to acknowledge their need for God. They become like the affluent farm family in Jane Smiley's novel *A Thousand Acres*. "We went to church to pay our respects, not to give thanks," remarks the narrator-daughter of a family that successfully farmed unpromising land with the benefit of hard work, innovation, and application of expensive technology. With all that who needs God?

In either case—times of extreme social and political distress, or times of security and affluence that distract people from a consciousness of their dependence on God—it is the saint who makes God reappear. Epiphany, therefore, occasions a reflection on the call to sanctity, to union with God, on the part of believers who are called to translate

Christmas "fantasy" (the word is etymologically linked to "epiphany") into the other fifty-one weeks of the year.

The original Epiphany event introduced gift-giving to the Nativity story, not necessarily to the celebration of Christmas as we know it (I'm not sure exactly when the custom of gift-exchange began), but to the New Testament narrative of the birth of Christ. With the Magi comes the suggestion that we are called to a balance in our lives between matter and spirit. The material side is surely represented in their gifts, particularly the gold. The spiritual is also there. It is exhibited first in their readiness to respond to divine direction, to follow the star. It is also contained in the symbolism of the gift of incense (prayer, homage, respect) and myrrh (a gum resin with a bitter taste, prefiguring the bitter death this child would suffer). Perhaps through a better balance of matter and spirit in contemporary Christian living, sanctity can become more evident in the world, thus enabling God to be seen a bit more clearly, to "reappear," in a manner of speaking, in our midst.

Isaiah's voice is heard again in the Epiphany liturgy: "Your light has come, the glory of the Lord shines upon you. See, darkness covers the earth, and thick clouds cover the peoples; but upon you the Light shines, and over you appears his glory" (Is 60:1-2). The words are repeated annually in the Epiphany liturgy because the Church wants you to hear them, and believe them, and apply them to yourself. "Upon *you* the Lord shines and over *you* appears his glory." Who can say whether or not the emphasis was there "in the original," as the editorial notation would put it? It probably was. It certainly should be to the eye and ear of faith today.

You may feel at this moment, now that the decorations are down and, perhaps, your spirits with them, that you are "walking in darkness." Or it may just be your stage in life or some troubling circumstance that has you down. You've got to believe that your Lord has broken through the darkness, dispersed the clouds, and is shining now on you. You now have the job of letting him shine through you to others. That is saints' work, and that is what you, as a Christian, are called to do.

Epiphany is a composite of two words: "epi" and "phano," meaning to shine forth, to let your light "bump up against" the world.

You hear the question occasionally, "Did the Magi really exist? Was there really a star?" A sensible reply is that no one knows for sure with historical precision, and, for that matter, the literal truth of the story is unimportant. There were in fact Babylonian or Chaldean "wise men" in those days; there were also Persian "wise men" at the time of the birth of Christ. They were respected as astronomers and as, what the gospel story calls, "astrologers."

The real question is: Why did the Holy Spirit want these elements included in the gospel story? What is the religious or theological purpose of the story of the Wise Men?

First, the story is there to stress the universality of Christ. He came not just to the Jews, but to the Gentiles (the *gentes*)—the other nations—as well. The gospel story has him "showing himself forth" to the nations. It is an epiphany. St. Matthew's gospel is also stressing the fact that Jesus is the messiah-king. The story thus serves the theological purpose of the author, and that, of course, is fine. But what about us? What about the question the writings of Matthew and Isaiah raises for you today? "Your light has come...Upon you the Lord shines."

Christ, the light of your life, is "out there," of course, in the world. But he is also within you. You have always to be setting out, as the Magi did, to find him. Yours is both an outward and an inward journey. You've got a star to follow. That star is your vocation; it is visible in the circumstances of your life, the circumstances that help you define or describe yourself—as husband or wife, father or mother, broker, lawyer, driver, manager, civil servant, teacher, volunteer, businessperson, nurse, physician, vowed religious, retiree—whatever the circumstances of your calling; that's your star, your vocation. It is a moving star because the God who calls never stops calling. You have to follow that call, that star, to find Christ your light, as the Magi did. And you find him only to pass him on, by word and example, to others.

As Christmas turns into Epiphany, and Epiphany reopens the door to "ordinary time" and ordinary life, you can consider anew your opportunity to be a saint, to let that little light of yours shine and brighten your corner of a troubled world. "It is the saint," as Lawrence Cunningham indicated, "who makes God reappear."

Epiphany!